G000149269

ORPHEUS

First published in 2018 by
The Dedalus Press
13 Moyclare Road
Baldoyle
Dublin D13 K1C2
Ireland

www.**dedaluspress**.com

ISBN 978 1 910251 30 0

Dedalus Press titles are represented in the UK by
Inpress Books, www.inpressbooks.co.uk,
and in North America by Syracuse University Press, Inc.,
www.syracuseuniversitypress.syr.edu.

Cover: Pat Boran

The Dedalus Press receives financial assistance from
The Arts Council / An Chomhairle Ealaíon.

ORPHEUS

THEO DORGAN

DEDALUS PRESS

ACKNOWLEDGEMENTS

Some of these poems or versions of them appeared in *fermata,* eds. Eva Bourke and Vincent Woods (Artisan House, Letterfrack, 2016).

CONTENTS

for Keith Payne and Su Garrido Pombo

PART 1

1

I stand back from the streetlight at her school gate,
I make myself invisible, blood pulsing
in raised veins. Exams are near, she's studying late.
My first brush with fate —

I am all attention, my nerves electric.
Breathing is difficult, couldn't answer to what
I am doing here; driven or drawn, can't tell which,
fear I might be sick...

These days, likely someone would call the police.
I'd stop myself, would take a careful look at
the staring boy, dense in his concentration,
so clearly obsessed —

and that was me at seventeen, some grey twist
in my head, shot through with fires of rage and hope,
gambling for my salvation on the one cool
glance I feared to miss.

2

Long hours in the attic under the bare slates,
teaching myself the moves, the bar chords, songs
I might somehow find the nerve to perform, sing
when the hour is late

in forgiving company. Don't let it slip,
keep cool, you can make this work, head down and rapt,
the phrase turned over and over, carving grooves
in my fingertips.

All that I needed was to play it out right,
sure that to reproduce was to make it true —
I thought discipline meant to rein myself back,
I'd stay up all night

if I had to, 'til I had it note-perfect —
conjuring what I ached for in the shadows,
imagining her stretched there in the dim light,
nodding her respect.

3

Pub door latched shut, somebody calls for hush,
the singer begins. My head's an open cave
and back in the dark the song takes root, shadows
writhe and twist and push

towards starlight, rise and fall back, called out, fearful,
called up to speak their pride. Sung, the song is old
but by this made new, all of us lost and quiet,
some of us tearful.

There by the fire, she has just come in, coat
flecked with rain, a fine mist in her hair. She turns,
unhoods her grey eyes, looks through the song at me.
Time dies in my throat.

I am away somehow to where the song starts
and sure of every breath I will take from now.
My shoulder down and forward, I part the crowd,
drawn to shadowed heart.

4

She sang *The Last Time I Saw Richard.* Joni
herself did not sing it so clean and so clear;
even the trad heads quietened, gave her respect.
Her voice was honey

in a glass of whiskey, cold as blue clear gin.
She finished her drink and left before applause
could kill the moment or the song. My heart
felt Richard walk in,

called up from wherever songs are born or go,
or some Richard who was myself — that was the
next thought to trouble my mind. I ached for what
I needed to know,

borne up on guesswork, the lifting tide of what
yet might be. Arguing philosophy by day,
sullen at night in company, often shunned —
deserved what I got.

5

Another night; someone hands me a guitar
and she sings out — a sideways look, a brief nod
and we're off and up into the swoop of it,
we are near and far,

voice following instrument, chords dipping
to underpin voice, my hands making shapes to
cup and lift whatever's moving there far down,
tremulous, climbing

out beyond her. She steps back inside herself
to let everyone else join in the chorus;
I keep the tune going, the bare bones of it,
gone into myself

but not to where she had gone, not there, not yet.
There was a fight and someone's nose got broken,
she'd left by then with some fool, a law student.
I slept on carpet.

6

In an ash grove on the side of a low hill
above the sea, camping with friends from college;
we sang and played, talked, laughed, argued, until the
fire had gone to ash.

Dark tents at intervals faced to the sea. Stars.
A girl half-known laid her thin hand on mine, said
come sleep with me tonight. I stood, stretched, followed.
When you play guitar,

she said, her head flung back, staring up at me,
when you play guitar I feel your hands move over
my breasts. I sensed the stars move over us
in a heavy wheel,

moved in my body sure as I moved in hers,
quickened and dense, airy and heavy all at
once. And then, fire slaked, we followed the night down
in tender murmurs.

7

A brief affair, a kindliness, had lifted
me into some grace. I became more myself
the more I played in company, I could learn
things from the gifted

among my new friends, and what I heard I could
put to use. Hands that had learned to give pleasure,
heart that had gained heart's ease, mind now more at peace,
in a better mood —

I had all I needed to make good. Or so
I thought. I gathered listeners, admirers,
found body companions drawn to the sessions,
sank into the glow,

became, as the saying goes, full of myself.
I might have died in my soul and not known it,
until I saw pity flash in those grey eyes.
She looked shook. Bereft.

8

That night I followed her, I'm ashamed to say;
shadow to doorway, a sly boy in the wet
streets, heart in mouth, a furtive driven thing in
the night's dip and sway.

On through the flat of the city, past the bars
with their babbling lights, gross noise and smells, and on
up along Summerhill, my hand trailing the
cold sandstone wall. Far

up into Mayfield I followed. To this day
I could not say what I feared or hoped to find.
She had walked out in the middle of some song,
her sharp cold disdain

had pierced me to the quick. I just could not bear
that slap of contempt. Between two dim streetlights,
slender figure grown compact of itself, she
simply disappeared.

9

I was trying out words, testing some slight gift
more sensed than believed; awkward, tentative things —
even then I knew they were no good.
My mind in a rift,

a narrow, a deep darkness. Could not read fate,
lived by night. I felt the walls were closing in.
Flicking the dictionary, scanning for signs,
I read: *Graduate* —

arranged in a series, marked out on a scale.
Took my degree in an absent-minded daze
but knew I was marking time; life was elsewhere,
I feared I might fail

in courage, fall into what was pre-ordained,
what was expected. Panicked, I bolted for
New York, possessed by a sudden need to break
for the outlaw plains.

10

Not a bad life, if you're up for it, young, brash,
bold and illegal: work in an Irish bar
by night and busk the days, friends or half-strangers
good for a month's crash —

I thrived on it, for a while. On Clinton Street,
floating home one winter night, I met myself
in a black bodega glass, my mirrored fetch
smack on the backbeat

of whatever I was humming. I went cold
to the bone, hard cold, the kind that stops your breath
and makes your heart contract. He stared me down,
a long look foretold

by some sense deep inside me. All this a fall
and fright-fail, a crash in trust, in what was known;
he knew, though, what and where I was. I did not
know myself at all.

11

Now I worked bars by day and played them by night.
Nothing like home, where tunes droned and rose against
the roar of drink, chaos and old spite. Here I'd
get something right

and be greeted with mild applause, a neat riff
or turn of phrase would be heard, is what I mean.
This always lifted me, made me want better.
Challenging my gift.

Sometimes, though, flatpicking my old guitar or
fitting a string to the machine head, I would
feel gone away inside; neither here nor there.
There was no horror

in this, no deep-struck fear — that was once only
though it never quite left me. Woke one morning
in someone's bed, said of myself quite calmly,
this man is lonely.

12

A friend wrote to say he had been in Brixton
to score some good dope, had seen her walk past, head
high as ever, stopping whenever that cold
grey eye would fix on

something of interest. Like an inspector,
he said, but of what I do not know — man, she
freaks me out, I can't for the life of me see
what you see in her.

You wouldn't, I thought, and never will either,
you and your dreary ballads and come all ye's,
could imagine him, too, jumping on a bus
just to avoid her.

Then my own cowardice rose in my throat like bile:
how far you ran, I accused myself, how far
you went to avoid your own deep-scribed desires —
this treason exile.

13

No sooner felt, understood, than forced under;
life is elsewhere, the voice inside insisted,
but I had an answer for that, I had learned
well how to plunder

sensation and accident for its balms and
soporifics, how to mine audiences
for cheap approval, how to make music out
of the second-hand

repertoire — soup of the soup, Sufis would say —
but little by little I felt the hesitation,
the stutter and gradual clouding over,
darkening my days.

Enough! *You need to leave.* Minnesota Jane
at breakfast one morning, pouring the coffee.
Go home, she said, *and don't come round here no more.*
Hudson river, dawn.

14

But where was home? Where they have to take you in?
I was channeling America full bore,
talk about Dylan —

I ask you! The man was everywhere you looked,
hard to believe there'd been a time when he was
grubbing the same East Village streets, just like us,
trying to get booked,

hustling for a gig, driven down on the wind
from the cold north country, the iron land up there.
And then, I saw. You can't go home, you take it
and make it legend

but you never go back, you press on into
the carnival night where the cold winds blow truths
of dust and fire into your aching heart, you
make the myth from you.

15

Somehow, I had let them down, this was made plain
in a half-averted look, a half-turned back
when I'd push in the door, guitar case in hand.
See you're back again,

New York too hot for you, was it? Played with Bob,
did you? Was he asking for us? More fool you,
I told myself, walking the lanes and the quays,
tired of having to fob

off sly welcome home, unfunny joke and jibe;
you knew to expect this, life in small cities,
everyone knowing everybody's business,
protecting the tribe.

You're full of shit, my sister said, when I cracked
and complained. *Everyone's hoping you'll make good,*
that's all in your head. Been up to see herself?
You know that she's back?

16

Well, and what kept you? Hand on the doorjamb,
black braids of hair falling to either side of
that narrow, high-cheeked face; her appraising gaze.
I said, here I am.

We let the moment flow back into the cave
of house behind her, the silence and darkness
of where she laid her head, made bread and music.
She held my look, grave

and considering. *Why did you never speak?*
No words, I suppose, I said, you know yourself.
I do, she said, thoughtful, and looked me in the eye.
I felt strong and weak

at the same time, a certain charge in the air.
A passing neighbor stopped to stare, then moved
on. Time was quick and slow. A hard wind came up.
She said, *now you're here.*

17

At one point in the night I heard a door slam,
started back on braced arms, alarmed. *My father,*
she said, gone still beneath; then, hand to my mouth,
doesn't give a damn.

I woke alone, panicked, a moment only
before I saw her at the window, black
fall of unbraided hair shimmering in the breeze.
I said, I'm lonely

here on my own, and she said without turning
you don't know what lonely is. Then she knelt down
beside the bed, took my face in her hands, said
Inside I'm burning,

do you understand? Static sparked in the air,
the curtains billowed. We washed and dressed, silent
and deft, quick. *Now,* she said, hefting a bag, *take*
me away from here.

18

Roscoff did not appeal, we made on for Rennes,
found a *chambre de bonne* on a quiet street near
the cathedral — it felt like we'd gone to ground,
that hounds and huntsmen

had cast into another field: a Lord's grave,
a witched field with high ditches and bright sharp thorns —
it seemed we'd fallen in with Tom O'Bedlam,
The Little Musgrave,

fatal women, blood-boltered faithless lovers,
world-circling sailors, half-rings in their purses —
a whole gallimaufry drawn from the ancient
marches and borders.

She had a predilection for the cards,
turned up The Hanged Man nine times in a row for
me, herself drew the Queen of Cups, convinced me
we were orphan wards.

19

I gave myself to her, a fall fuelled by need.
Deep in her aura of turbulent dreams at night,
in the strong air she inhabited by day,
I never paid heed

to the small warnings that flashed up in my mind,
the darts of unease, quick doubts, hesitations
at something she might say or do. I was
somehow of her kind,

that's all I knew — at least that's what I believed,
or needed to believe, wanted to think true.
Sometimes it was all too much for me,
this dark energy,

but I fed on it, too, felt the roots of day
stirred and disturbed, untwisting, to search blind
tips ever downward into the old, hard ground,
down to the cold clay.

20

We rose each day, ate a silent breakfast, then
headed out, still unspeaking, to teach guitar,
piano. Work led to work, we had acquired
by that summer's end

a reputation for results. Criss-crossing
the city we were preoccupied, absorbed,
would barely speak if we met — nobody could
say we were dossing

but we were getting nowhere. This can't go on,
I heard myself say, we were making dinner,
the skylights propped open to let the steam out.
We should abandon

this? Over her shoulder, neck locked and tense.
This, meaning us, our made life together here.
No, I said, look at me. Now, see what I mean?
Night fell on silence.

21

The trouble is, I've always known what I want.
And I knew, I said, I always wanted you.
First time I saw you, the pub, that time I sang,
you heard the descant…

You knew I was there, those cold nights after school…
No, listen, I mean the first time I saw you…
Now there was static in the air, no time to
hide, to play the fool —

Exactly. I knew right then I wanted you.
No, listen, not just to fuck, or hold, or have,
though that's all good; it's good, this life we make here.
You heard what was true

in the song, you knew the form, saw how it meant;
you heard the old call, the song under the song.
Weeping now, beyond all consoling: *You don't*
give me what I want.

22

I never met more capable musician,
could turn her hand to keyboard and wind alike;
favoured the harpsichord, the flute — Scarlatti,
Bach and Couperin,

notes flowed from her fingers as plectrum plucked wire,
spiky, melodious, fluent, all got out
in their feathered skeletons, phrase winged to phrase —
she could fly higher

and fall far faster than anyone I know.
I'd sat by the door one winter in a church,
unseen by her, I made sure, and heard her out.
She could make it flow —

I slipped away behind loud walls of applause,
down Winter's Hill, a thick filigree of frost
whitening the slates of Sunday's Well — just, she
followed all the laws.

23

We ran for Paris, fled in the dark of night,
the wind thundering around the slate rooftops;
fled in a gale like outlaws before some Lord
and his vengeful might.

Wrapped in a warm cloak, her face made pale by grief,
she was the doomed maid forlorn, cast up from sea
on storm-tossed rocks, on a hostile, foreign shore
and I was the thief

of dreams, the wily, resourceful, slender lad
from the greenwoods, minstrel and warrior true,
who'd bring her to treasure and to her heart's ease ...
I know it sounds mad,

and we weren't tripping, nor even that stoned,
but we needed a narrative to drive us,
needed a story. Place de la République,
black coffee at dawn.

24

Horses for courses, my Granda liked to say —
I took to Paris and Paris took to me.
Someone who'd heard me play in New York, chance met
on the Quai d'Orsay,

offered a residency in a club he
part-owned, helped us to find a small apartment,
one night brought by to listen, he said, a friend —
he makes the records,

small independent label, you know, good taste —
and the friend liked what he heard, I had a deal,
went to work on songs. All these years, nothing, it
seemed, had gone to waste.

I felt the fates were gathering in the threads
of all I had been and done. I felt set free,
doors were opening on all sides. I had what
I thought I wanted.

25

Once and once only she came to hear me. Months
had gone by and if I thought I was happy,
I did not know that she was not. Now we shared
space, a roof, where once

we had shared a life. I was all attention
to myself, enthralled by gift; I say it now,
I was cruel and crass in my uncaring,
starry dimensions

and ordinary human grace alike all
lost to me. I was burning with ego — this
I admit, and I do not forgive myself.
I made a bad call

and I carry the fault yet. No working through
can unmake the past. On the way home she said
you have them now but, though you don't see it yet,
now, now they have you.

26

She bought a bentside spinet at a market,
had it repaired and tuned. Once, wearing only high
boots, bent over the keyboard, she had me take
her in the dark, it

was blunt, brief, impersonal. Such howl she gave
at the end. And then, wordless, she showered, dressed
and walked out. Gone for days. I could no longer
understand her ways.

I've always thought heaven would be a cold place
she said one day, swaying and dipping where the
shadow of Sacré Coeur lay on the pavement;
epiphany, grace

of an unexpected kind. Just then, just there,
she had air under her feet. *I've never thought
I'll make old bones,* she said, stopped. Her face a mask,
hand sweeping her hair.

27

Someone I met by chance brought news of home, had
heard I was *doing well,* was avid to hear, see
what the story was. Stayed on after the show.
I heard that her Dad

died, he said, *she didn't make it home?* Didn't know —
I was brusque, had almost forgotten that lust
to unsettle, to take while seeming to give,
sly innuendo

their stock in trade. Fuck you, I thought, left him there
at the bar. She was asleep, I did not want
to wake her. When I asked, she just shrugged, left it
hanging in the air.

As with so much between us. Pain marked our days
now, a strained silence the best we could manage.
Rages, of course, torrents of scalding words. *I'm
always in your way.*

28

A rocket was launching from Cape Kennedy,
I was watching TV, slow parabola
of the breakaway as the booster stage
fell back to earth. She

came in the door, a fine mist in her long hair,
saw what I was looking at, went suddenly
pale, reached for my face, crushed it between her hands;
something in that stare

unnerved me, that long, unblinking gaze went straight
down inside me, a cold hand searching to wrench
something free. Afraid to move or even breathe,
I thought brooding hate

had overtaken her until her eyes went
soft, her hands relented and some terminal
sorrow broke like a wave in the room; we wept
until we were spent.

29

Métro Saint-Michel. Everything much too loud
after a day of silence by the river.
At the interchange I plunge out, unheeding,
shouldering through crowds

to the far escalator. I turn, look back,
she's stood there looking up, deep wells of sorrow
in her eyes. From the turbulent crowd she signs
I just can't go on.

Hard fluorescent light, waterfall of black noise,
then a fainting away of all except
that resolute, beseeching figure. Her
unbearable poise.

I batter my way down, panic-struck, fearing
the worst. A loud hiss, the sound of doors closing,
rumbling rubber wheels, light on the last carriage
red, vanishing, gone.

30

Three days and three nights I walked the apartment,
pacing it out, numbering all that was lost.
I was ghost to myself, shadowed and hollow,
everything there bent

into a downward spiral —rooms, the city,
all we had been and the incoherent dreams
we had failed to spell out right, now never would ...
electricity

spat from everything I touched, my nerves so raw
I could not bear the feel of clothes on my skin.
Rancid, unwashed, I prowled like a driven thing
from window to wall,

wall to window, muttering and gesturing
to the foetid air. And then it all just, stopped.
Like that. Silence, a vast composure settling.
I heard her voice: *Sing*.

31

Three days and nights I worked in a frenzy, paced
and stood frozen, chasing the tune, the phrases,
the notes and chords. The hardest was to find words
of adequate grace

and weight. I saw I had learned my craft but not
how to trust myself on the long plunge into
chaos, what can be found there, named and brought back.
That was a hard-fought

war — I wept, sweated, swore, built and tore back down
version and version, but I did it. I made
her song, and made my name. It keeps itself, it
stands on common ground.

In the long years after, I would hear it played,
sung, in so many voices I could forget
it was mine, could hope she might hear, accept it
as debt fully paid.

32

That song did well for me, and I did well after —
concerts, recordings, a following, enough
to give me a decent life; much of this owed
to my manager.

Good friends gave more, taught me how to keep my head:
the money, the brief affairs, of course the drugs —
we all know how that goes: first you burn bright,
then you fall down dead.

And yet, and yet there are times when I walk out
into the night, in some half-known city, fall off
the known map of the touring life, away from
the after-party rout,

the closed-mouth venue manager, the old friends
come backstage — I walk the streets down until dawn,
desperate for one more cold challenging glance
before this life ends.

33

The long decades passed; I did my work, I did
what good I could, all over the turning world.
I learned, of course you can go home again, found
that time parsed and sieved

will yield gold if you're patient. Friends of my youth
have not forgot me, my city is mine still
although I can't live there. I hear on the wind
that she made it through,

is out there in the world; I'm thankful to her.
What was for me always found me in the end.
The fates put a good companion in my way —
we have a daughter

with steady eyes who sang at her mother's breast.
I work the old trade as many have before,
I play the cards I'm dealt. I hope to die old,
grateful, doing my best.

PART 2

1

Tender they nursed me, cradled my severed head,
circling in moonlight under the spreading oak,
passed me from hand to hand, kissing my eyelids.
Called up from the dead.

Wind buffeted the moon, vault of stars above
wheeled with the night's passage. They sang until dawn
flushed on the sea below. Song bird started up
from deep in the grove,

note borrowed note, song gave me breath, breath gave bone,
gave start, made quick. I stood before them, half blind,
staggered into the chorus, naked and cold —
knew myself alone

for all that sweet company, their generous gift
of song and life again, their blithe disinterest.
The woods took them; the wind gathered force, I gave
myself to that lift.

2

Horsemen in the valley below, high clear air
all around me on the sun-cracked crags. Unseen,
cousin to eagle, I watch them drive the game.
Height makes me severe,

my mind moves on judgement, on memory.
These thoughts displease the god, threaten his favour:
what's past is past, dismemberment undone, the
women, that story,

gone to the clouds of night, embers of firelight —
shadowplay of the tale-tellers, old men
who record and invent to beguile day, to
people fearful night.

I scan the braided rivers, lifted here to
search out the places where willows grow, sacred
to Helike, necessary to me. The god
lets these horsemen go.

3

Alder is rampant, willow takes the field, reeds
bend in their golden acres by riverbank.
I let the old flute fall, I make one new, find
always what I need

and find myself again. Bird notes ring out clear,
now flute weaving follows, threading the hollow
groves, floating out over the silver rivers.
What was far, now near.

Old skills, old bones made new — I doubt my old art
and yet walk out, morning after morning, sure
that the path can be trusted, that now remade
I know my own part

in this retelling. The women made me new,
the stones that tranced out of memory dance now
and trees lift up their arms to know that, up here,
every thing rings true.

4

There in the path, bright morning, a tortoise shell.
Gift of the dryads, the god? Hardly. I looked
down and east to where a lone eagle circled
bare rock by a well,

heard as bones cracked and he plunged for the marrow —
the wind-lifted shell made soundbox for my lyre,
willow and skilled knifecraft gave arms and crossbars,
stag-gut strung my bow

after a long, sweaty chase had brought him down.
Thus art — chance, craft and butchery, nature's gift,
all spun together in a whirl of making
by one who had drowned,

was dismembered, surfaced whole again to sing.
I saw what I had made, and found it was good;
settled soon after against a fire-warmed wall
I let the notes ring.

5

Falcons — I watch them stoop, shoot upward, thwarted.
Again and again. Hover, survey, then strike.
Down in the undergrowth small things twist and run —
mostly they escape.

Such terror in small hearts, such desperate swerve
and turn, panic, white light and breath near undone —
I feel myself project, lock, hold and retreat,
strain in every nerve,

fetching this new understanding back to thought.
Always before I had seen myself as hawk —
circling, then plunging down from the high serene
to pluck out the note

from among the roots and add it to my string.
Now everything's upside down and inside out,
I see it is not the sweeping hand that plays
but the notes that sing.

6

Stopping by woods while climbing to my outlook
I felt my cheek caressed, my blood run cold.
A rank gust, a crash deep in the grove, the ground
under my feet shook.

For days the god had not been near, I was all
discord and out of sorts, choleric and sad
and glad of my solitude. And now, out of
the deep woods, a call

from the known place, world I thought I had forgot —
a rippling silver phrase rang in the birchleaves,
underscored by a grunt, a staccato cough ...
I dropped the clay pot

I had been carrying, snatched up a wet shard
and scratched on a flat rock the fugitive notes
already dying on the wind. A sea breeze
rose and hit me hard.

7

Lyre on the ridges, hand sweeping the bright strings
like waves making towards the sun-white shore below.
Pipe in the pine grove, breath so easy and clear
the new tune takes wing.

Sleep deep in the cave, wrapped in bear skin, wolf pelt
folded under my head. The god sent me dreams,
the stars in the cave mouth if I woke early
scribed out what I felt —

crane scratch and glyph, thin sharp notations of
a point scratching across the infinite sky.
Waking and sleeping I felt myself swung
between mark and strophe,

as if something or someone was writing me
out on the screens of night and day. I kept sane
by keeping score: pipe in the mountain grove,
lyre notes down to sea.

8

Back in the long before, I was enchanter —
and arrogant with the gift. I could make stones
move, men made me famous for it with their talk,
muttered *sorcerer*

as I passed, silently crowding to my heels —
and I confess I liked it, the awe they felt
a kind of sustaining echo to my own,
cold air to anneal

the blade of thought. Now I am found enchanted,
the song sings me & gives me pause. The god intends
this, such has been made known. Reborn in silence,
I have recanted

belief in my power, surrendered my one art
to itself. By sea, by cliff, by woods I walk,
tending the busy music of what happens,
entranced with my part.

9

Down in the villages I know they hear me,
how could they not? These builders of terrace walls,
tenders of vine, crop and flock, charcoal makers —
diligent, busy

people. I admire them, keep myself apart
all the same, can feel kinship without
needing to be among kind. Mine is not a
solitary art,

that's what I mean to say, and if they can hear me
when I play, they hear it all. Hesitant starts,
blank silence, whole liquid runs, I give it all —
I can let it be

and so can they. Learning again how to play
as a child would, fingering without forethought,
not careless and not unconscious, just keeping
out of my own way.

10

What was required? Do not imagine I did
not demand this — of the god, the night, the vast
expanse of sky, mountain, plain and sea below.
Not that it was hid

from me, I did not imagine that, but lacked
understanding of how I might understand.
Just so. I was the season's hunter and the
self-same game he tracked,

bent to blind purpose I sensed but could not know.
I had my instruments, my gift intact, my
store of technique, my basic needs all cared for —
and nothing to show

for it: hale, healthy, reborn on that cold shore,
I knew that more was required, I could see that —
why else should the fates have made me whole again,
made my heart so sore?

11

I loved her, but not enough. Blunt and cold,
the thought full-formed struck like electric bolt hurled
from a deep, dark grove. Stopped me in my tracks.
I felt my spine fold,

collapse, a thick mist came into my head and
I fell down. When I came to, my mouth was stopped
with dust. My pipe lay shattered, I'd fallen
awkward on my hand.

A stream chattered and sang clear near by. I crawled
towards the sound, did not know where I was or who
I might be. Or, for that matter, what. I looked
back where I lay sprawled

and wondered at his case. Pain racked in my bones,
I spasmed and gasped, he jerked, jolted, tried to stand —
something untoward shook and took me. Light fled,
I lay there alone.

12

The fates found me, they nursed me back to the world.
A white wolf lay at my feet, his yellow eyes
thoughtful, unblinking. An oriole called from
the grove, green leaves whirled

in a small vortex of dust and brushed my face.
My damaged hand lay in the running water,
I knew it would heal; I would make a new reed.
I made myself brace

and stand. No broken bones. Such swift accounting
of my state, such clarity of thought, was not
natural — this I knew. Suddenly I felt
some terror mounting,

sweeping towards me from far down there below —
then a hawk crashed, brash, black, down from the cold heights,
breast feathers puffed up right before my eyes.
I let my fear go.

13

Something had opened up, some light-filled void
in my chest. I had lungs for hard climbing now,
legs that allowed me long range by day and night.
Even when I tried

to sit still, to sink down into listening,
this antic energy would not let me rest.
I loved her but not enough. I covered ground,
sweat glistening

on my brow, I loped with the wolf, ran frantic
with the deer and sometimes, cold-eyed and deadly
as Artemis, I hunted both. Words hunted me,
urgent and mantic,

words that I knew would never find a right air
until the god or my own fate would disclose
what was deep hid. Yet, I pride myself on this:
I did not despair.

14

Some shrewd discomfort made me keep high. Dryads
kept company with me on birch-bright ridges,
their fine laughter a comfort, a soothing balm;
their sister naiads

and all that palaver of the sea was lost
to me, nothing to draw down to that grave of
ships, haunt of drowned voyagers — or so I thought.
Then an early frost

brought to mind white lacework on a swollen sea
when the wind was getting up and a long fetch
would send fishermen racing for safe haven.
Salt voices called me

come down and down I went to Poseidon's brides,
those bright, teasing spirits — seized with sea-longing,
aware I had been bereft, aware of need,
putting grief aside.

15

What's for you will find you, a wise woman said,
full of the music herself, her clear shrewd eyes
coming back to me now, stars from the long-lost
skies inside my head.

Leaving the rocky crags all draped in sunlight,
coming down through the resiny groves, crossing
the grazed uplands, threading down through terraces,
I thought that I might

die down here, might fade again into the grey
airs and shadows, the null of what lay beyond
white ramparts of silent houses, shingle beach,
clouds across the bay.

I searched each face I met for some sign of threat
or promise, met their quiet courtesy with
a shy averted face — and was accepted.
Hail fellow, well met.

16

Hardworking people, I watched them come and go,
in and out of the narrow lanes, back and forth
from the neat, small harbour. I saw they watched me, too.
I made myself slow

in my movements, let my shoulders fall; I did
not want to draw more than a fair attention,
did not want to stand out. I let my hands show.
I was a shepherd,

I said easily, answering a blunt
question from a man who stood square in my path;
up there, a vague wave to the heights behind me.
Work is what I want.

I could do with a man — I turned as they laughed,
a small knot of women, one there who was tall
and frank, long black hair cascading to cocked hip.
I was hooked and gaffed.

17

Rhea, her name was, grey eyes forceful and cool.
Kept a taverna and kept good order, too.
I was for manhandling barrels, heavy work,
tasks that any fool

could manage with ease, holding his mind at bay.
I had a room that looked out over the sea,
a flat roof where I'd sit before night, watching
the hawks fall and sway

high on the darkening ridges up above.
The god had gone away, no prompt in the heart
to unsettle me without warning, no start
from the deep, dark grove

to set my blood rushing, no fears, no cold sweats —
and no music. That was a sweet, soft release.
t pleased me, brought ease to my days.
I had ceased to fret.

18

Nothing is forever — the great sway of things
through the cosmos in a dance that never stops,
men circling the world about their business, wild
creatures, birds that sing

when the light comes back, children as rooms grow dark,
mothers whose daughters give birth scarce-born themselves ...
I was adrift on slow whorls of heavy thought,
unwilling to mark

time — trying to fit in and at the same time
hold myself apart. *Some shepherd, that fella,*
I overheard a farmer say. *Something on
his mind — I'd say crime*

of passion, looks the type. Difference does that,
I found, engenders malice in simple folk,
but I had no art to hide from his cold thought,
that poisoned dart.

19

The world gives what you ask for, another law
that came back to me as day came to a close
and the lamps were lit. I was fearful again —
myself, what I saw

when I followed where music led, what my mind
disclosed to itself, what sounded in my heart.
I loved her but not enough. I thought the god
intended to be kind,

as the women were who had drawn me from
Lethe's waters, re-membered me on this earth;
but time out of mind flows on like a river
and every atom

that ever was returns in a higher round
to the same line through the vortex, then plunges
back down through dark void of chaos. No escape,
I was what I found.

20

I worked as required, diligent and as meek
as I could make myself be — who had been world-
girdling, who had made stone sound, tree dip and dance,
who had been to Greek

mind first father of sweet plaint, strophe, and measure.
I worked at my duties, spoke plain as I could
when spoken to, otherwise kept silent. Was
unlooked-for treasure,

she said, Rhea — whose eye sometimes fell on me
with a depth of thought behind her look
that would have shook me once. I kept my head down;
that was the only

refuge I had in that small place: avert my
gaze, refuse compact of eye from soul to soul.
That I was hiding something, she surely knew —
but she did not pry.

21

Rebel against myself, I laboured by night
and day, sweating the weary grind, glad of it,
thinking myself well hid in simple work, hid
in broad daylight,

but vulnerable to what moved in the dark,
shadows and presences in the room and deep
inside. Sometimes the hunt would sweep down through the
woods, the bay and bark

of it, horn-sounding tempest, flurry and crash
driving upset, troubled unease, before its
fury. Long after the village had settled
into the backwash,

a flock of birds settling their feathers, the leaves
falling still again in the noonday heat, I'd
feel my heart flexing to find ease in its cage,
struggling hard to breathe.

22

When the dark well of quiet inside became
unbearable I would ask her for time off.
She'd jerk her chin, turn away, as if to say
Go the way you came.

Up through the terraces over the shining cove,
up through the ravines and across the grazing
into the woods, the voice of the sea annulled
in the sighing grove.

Ring doves and orioles, soft push of a breeze
in the undergrowth hush, dryad skirts rustling
the brittle birch leaves, and somewhere up above
(I'd fall to my knees

in gratitude) the high impersonal call
of the hunting hawk. There I'd immerse myself
in healing silence, made sick below by talk.
Here I could stand tall.

23

Up here I can come to myself, I can heal.
Springs of clear water in a bright rock hollow,
I float in the living waters, see what light
chooses to reveal

in the fold and fall of the mountain draining
all away, down to the world of men below —
and am unmoved, peer like a cold immortal
from above, craning

to see what the antic doomed ones will do next.
And the music comes back, full flood: heft and sway,
broad chorus, the rising treble that never
will repeat, sacred text

of the word that masters chaos, cancels fears ...
and myself the agent and instrument, ward
of the god — made strong, made whole again, yes, but
doubt is always near.

24

After I'd slip back unseen, unheard, arrive
by night, surprised that the village dogs did not
track my way downhill, signal my shy return.
Next morning I'd dive

into the work, speaking to none, like someone
whose dream still held him back from the waking world.
Always the same response from her: soon after
the day had begun

she'd stand in the door, blocking my way, looking
over me at something out to sea. Some woman
passing would say, I see he's back. *Ah yes,
he missed my cooking.*

All this as if I were not there. On purpose,
of course, to teach me my place — or so I thought
until I understood: she feared she'd lost me
to the wilderness.

25

A blood moon rose into the warm air over
the flat, whispering sea. I watched it float up
into a broad-cast net of glinting stars, now
buoyant and silver,

and saw that the matrix had shifted, my frame
for the world and what happens there become that
of the sea-people, fishers by lantern light.
Hooked and gaffed, words came

to mind I had long forgot. All that long night
I sat by the shore, neither warm nor cold, there
and not there, letting halls of silence open
to whatever might

come. I was between worlds when the god returned.
Up on the heights I saw the sheet-lightning flash
through the frames that hold the world in its old place.
And now the sea burned.

26

I did not sleep that night. I took a boat out
before dawn, leaned on the bare wood of the oars
as if stone filled my arms, and when the early
risers were about

the day's business, stick figures in the pearly
glare, I stripped and went headfirst over the side
into shocking cold waters; my heart near stopped,
I very nearly

drowned — no, that's not true but almost I forgot
breath, surfaced into an empty glow of mind,
quivering and tense, alive and glad of this
life that was my lot.

Last night I had a thought, she said, her grey eyes
considering me, there on the shore. I stood
straight. *And the thought was this: we need a garden.*
That was a surprise.

27

Seven terraces, climbing the slope. Walls first,
a stone at a time, the hands learning heft and
fit until each flat rock seemed to flow at
its own pace, a burst

of blind energy at the start easing to
smooth pace as the days followed on, fluent grace
falling into place; her hands to my hands, sure,
slow, settled, and true.

Start in the half-light before dawn, the sky clear,
working down from the great cairn as the first birds
start to call from tree to tree. Easier to
carry down from there

than carry up, she'd said, and not for the first
time (or the last) I admired her common sense.
We found no need to speak, companionable,
thoughtful and immersed.

28

She was tireless, rangy and strong, unbothered,
methodical. Ingenious, too. Channelled
a spring from the grazing above to a vat
fed down to others

in a stepped cascade. One day I suddenly
understood that work is a music all its
own. Work and the silence around it, the pause
in the melody

and then the beat resumed. I heard a sharp crack
as if something had ruptured inside my head,
and fell straight down. She was bent over me when
I came, dizzy, back

to the world, her hair a tent on either side
of my head, her face so close I could feel my
soul drawn effortlessly upward into those
fathomless cool eyes.

29

Long, black hair is a flare of glory, banner
in spume on the sea shore, lifted on the breeze
or hung in a long coil between shoulder blades,
oiled in the manner

of those who live with salt in the air. Woman
poised at bleached shutters, examining something
of interest far out to sea, something or,
it may be, someone.

I was that someone, settling point of view
told me, smoke in her hair, low fire in the room
a faint cloudiness in the air; I hung
between known and new,

familiar and unfamiliar to myself.
Drink, she said, cradling my head, you had a fall.
Rough rug on skin, cold and heat. A votive of
Hermes on the shelf.

30

Recovered, I'd work beside her, day after
day, steadily breaking ground, setting out plants,
bedding them in. Sometimes we'd stand, gaze at the
black mountains: weather

up there, I'd say; heavy-banked clouds grey and black
on the high ridges, wind tossing the massed holm
groves, the sentinel pines. Or we'd turn seaward,
straightening our backs,

and she'd point out some gathering squall, small fleet
of fishing boats making for shelter. Between
large worlds, the small world we had made — tilled, damp earth,
green drifts at our feet.

I thought the bees were like handfuls of stray motes,
drifting on the breeze, until I saw patterns
of meaning emerge, heard and then saw music
in those glancing notes.

31

I lay on my back, a starfish, softly borne
up on warm night water, held out to the stars,
perseids quietly streaming through the sky,
a glinting bee swarm,

a shoal of patterning notes. Walls of the cove
gave back the heat of day, gave scent to the salt air.
I loved her but not enough — the thought came soft
through the night above,

settled clear in my mind. Euridike, dear
one, I see now where I went wrong, what I failed
to understand, then and since. When I stood there,
watched you disappear,

took death inside, it was my pride that ruled me
and not my heart. I thought you mine, thought I owed
and owned you, did not see you had made your choice.
Dear heart, forgive me.

32

She stood in the doorway, shadow against sky
bright with stars, lamplight picking out runnels and
hollows, the folds in her simple dress. I rose,
did not ask her why

now, after all this time, she had come. I knew.
Leaf-smoke in the air, harvest, full plenty; grave
joy, heartfelt words, plain talk, we rose into the
night, we soared, we flew

high beyond anywhere we had ever been
and yet stayed in body that had known body
in the long day's work; we were ourselves, made free
of what we had been.

And then, at the full end of all, soft and clear
as day she said *I've always known who you are,*
sing me a laughing daughter, sing me a child
who will know no fear.

33

The village enjoyed a day and night of mirth
at our expense — everyone saw it coming,
it seems, except us — *I could do with a man*
indeed! The prompt birth

of the girl saw me absorbed into the life
of the place for good. The god abandoned me
with a final grace note, my pipe and lyre laid
beside pruning knife

on the votive shelf. Once, looking at hawks climb
and circle on a high draft, a flight of seagulls
drifting up into the same music, she said
up there's out of time

but when you need to, go. And never you fear,
I'll reel you back when you're ready for our air.
Then the child smiled with her mother's cool grey eyes,
lifted free and clear.